MONEY LEDGER
FOR KIDS

BELONGS TO:

_____

STARTING BALANCE:

DATE	DESCRIPTION	MONEY SPENT	MONEY RECEIVED	BALANCE

NOTES: _____

_____

_____

_____

STARTING BALANCE:

DATE	DESCRIPTION	MONEY SPENT	MONEY RECEIVED	BALANCE

NOTES: _____

_____

_____

_____

STARTING BALANCE:

DATE	DESCRIPTION	MONEY SPENT	MONEY RECEIVED	BALANCE

NOTES: _____
_____
_____
_____

STARTING BALANCE: _____

DATE	DESCRIPTION	MONEY SPENT	MONEY RECEIVED	BALANCE

NOTES: _____

_____

_____

_____

STARTING BALANCE:

DATE	DESCRIPTION	MONEY SPENT	MONEY RECEIVED	BALANCE

NOTES: _____

_____

_____

_____

STARTING BALANCE:

DATE	DESCRIPTION	MONEY SPENT	MONEY RECEIVED	BALANCE

NOTES: _____

_____

_____

_____

STARTING BALANCE:

DATE	DESCRIPTION	MONEY SPENT	MONEY RECEIVED	BALANCE

NOTES: _____
_____
_____
_____

STARTING BALANCE:

DATE	DESCRIPTION	MONEY SPENT	MONEY RECEIVED	BALANCE

NOTES: _____

_____

_____

_____

STARTING BALANCE:

DATE	DESCRIPTION	MONEY SPENT	MONEY RECEIVED	BALANCE

NOTES: _____

_____

_____

_____

STARTING BALANCE:

DATE	DESCRIPTION	MONEY SPENT	MONEY RECEIVED	BALANCE

NOTES: _____
_____
_____
_____

STARTING BALANCE:

DATE	DESCRIPTION	MONEY SPENT	MONEY RECEIVED	BALANCE

NOTES: _____

_____

_____

_____

STARTING BALANCE:

DATE	DESCRIPTION	MONEY SPENT	MONEY RECEIVED	BALANCE

NOTES: _____

_____

_____

_____

STARTING BALANCE:

DATE	DESCRIPTION	MONEY SPENT	MONEY RECEIVED	BALANCE

NOTES: _____

_____

_____

_____

STARTING BALANCE: _____

DATE	DESCRIPTION	MONEY SPENT	MONEY RECEIVED	BALANCE

NOTES: _____

_____

_____

_____

STARTING BALANCE:

DATE	DESCRIPTION	MONEY SPENT	MONEY RECEIVED	BALANCE

NOTES: _____
_____
_____
_____

STARTING BALANCE:

DATE	DESCRIPTION	MONEY SPENT	MONEY RECEIVED	BALANCE

NOTES: _____
_____
_____
_____

STARTING BALANCE:

DATE	DESCRIPTION	MONEY SPENT	MONEY RECEIVED	BALANCE

NOTES: _____
_____
_____
_____

STARTING BALANCE: _____

DATE	DESCRIPTION	MONEY SPENT	MONEY RECEIVED	BALANCE

NOTES: _____

_____

_____

_____

STARTING BALANCE:

DATE	DESCRIPTION	MONEY SPENT	MONEY RECEIVED	BALANCE

NOTES: _____
_____
_____
_____

STARTING BALANCE:

DATE	DESCRIPTION	MONEY SPENT	MONEY RECEIVED	BALANCE

NOTES: _____

_____

_____

_____

STARTING BALANCE:

DATE	DESCRIPTION	MONEY SPENT	MONEY RECEIVED	BALANCE

NOTES: _____
_____
_____
_____

STARTING BALANCE: _____

DATE	DESCRIPTION	MONEY SPENT	MONEY RECEIVED	BALANCE

NOTES: _____

_____

_____

_____

STARTING BALANCE:

DATE	DESCRIPTION	MONEY SPENT	MONEY RECEIVED	BALANCE

NOTES: _____

_____

_____

_____

STARTING BALANCE:

DATE	DESCRIPTION	MONEY SPENT	MONEY RECEIVED	BALANCE

NOTES: _____
_____
_____
_____

STARTING BALANCE:

DATE	DESCRIPTION	MONEY SPENT	MONEY RECEIVED	BALANCE

NOTES: _____

_____

_____

_____

STARTING BALANCE:

DATE	DESCRIPTION	MONEY SPENT	MONEY RECEIVED	BALANCE

NOTES: _____

_____

_____

_____

STARTING BALANCE:

DATE	DESCRIPTION	MONEY SPENT	MONEY RECEIVED	BALANCE

NOTES: _____
_____
_____
_____

STARTING BALANCE:

DATE	DESCRIPTION	MONEY SPENT	MONEY RECEIVED	BALANCE

NOTES: _____

_____

_____

_____

STARTING BALANCE: _____

DATE	DESCRIPTION	MONEY SPENT	MONEY RECEIVED	BALANCE

NOTES: _____

_____

_____

_____

STARTING BALANCE:

DATE	DESCRIPTION	MONEY SPENT	MONEY RECEIVED	BALANCE

NOTES: _____

_____

_____

_____

STARTING BALANCE:

DATE	DESCRIPTION	MONEY SPENT	MONEY RECEIVED	BALANCE

NOTES: _____

_____

_____

_____

STARTING BALANCE:

DATE	DESCRIPTION	MONEY SPENT	MONEY RECEIVED	BALANCE

NOTES: _____

_____

_____

_____

STARTING BALANCE:

DATE	DESCRIPTION	MONEY SPENT	MONEY RECEIVED	BALANCE

NOTES: _____
_____
_____
_____

STARTING BALANCE:

DATE	DESCRIPTION	MONEY SPENT	MONEY RECEIVED	BALANCE

NOTES: _____
_____
_____
_____

STARTING BALANCE:

DATE	DESCRIPTION	MONEY SPENT	MONEY RECEIVED	BALANCE

NOTES: _____
_____
_____
_____

STARTING BALANCE:

DATE	DESCRIPTION	MONEY SPENT	MONEY RECEIVED	BALANCE

NOTES: _____
_____
_____
_____

STARTING BALANCE:

DATE	DESCRIPTION	MONEY SPENT	MONEY RECEIVED	BALANCE

NOTES: _____

_____

_____

_____

STARTING BALANCE: _____

DATE	DESCRIPTION	MONEY SPENT	MONEY RECEIVED	BALANCE

NOTES: _____

_____

_____

_____

STARTING BALANCE:

DATE	DESCRIPTION	MONEY SPENT	MONEY RECEIVED	BALANCE

NOTES: _____
_____
_____
_____

STARTING BALANCE:

DATE	DESCRIPTION	MONEY SPENT	MONEY RECEIVED	BALANCE

NOTES: _____

_____

_____

_____

STARTING BALANCE:

DATE	DESCRIPTION	MONEY SPENT	MONEY RECEIVED	BALANCE

NOTES: _____

_____

_____

_____

STARTING BALANCE:

DATE	DESCRIPTION	MONEY SPENT	MONEY RECEIVED	BALANCE

NOTES: _____

_____

_____

_____

STARTING BALANCE:

DATE	DESCRIPTION	MONEY SPENT	MONEY RECEIVED	BALANCE

NOTES: _____

_____

_____

_____

STARTING BALANCE:

DATE	DESCRIPTION	MONEY SPENT	MONEY RECEIVED	BALANCE

NOTES: _____

_____

_____

_____

STARTING BALANCE:

DATE	DESCRIPTION	MONEY SPENT	MONEY RECEIVED	BALANCE

NOTES: _____

_____

_____

_____

STARTING BALANCE:

DATE	DESCRIPTION	MONEY SPENT	MONEY RECEIVED	BALANCE

NOTES: _____
_____
_____
_____

STARTING BALANCE:

DATE	DESCRIPTION	MONEY SPENT	MONEY RECEIVED	BALANCE

NOTES: _____

_____

_____

_____

STARTING BALANCE:

DATE	DESCRIPTION	MONEY SPENT	MONEY RECEIVED	BALANCE

NOTES: _____

_____

_____

_____

STARTING BALANCE:

DATE	DESCRIPTION	MONEY SPENT	MONEY RECEIVED	BALANCE

NOTES: _____
_____
_____
_____

STARTING BALANCE: _____

DATE	DESCRIPTION	MONEY SPENT	MONEY RECEIVED	BALANCE

NOTES: _____

_____

_____

_____

STARTING BALANCE:

DATE	DESCRIPTION	MONEY SPENT	MONEY RECEIVED	BALANCE

NOTES: _____

_____

_____

_____

STARTING BALANCE:

DATE	DESCRIPTION	MONEY SPENT	MONEY RECEIVED	BALANCE

NOTES:_____

_____

_____

_____

STARTING BALANCE:

DATE	DESCRIPTION	MONEY SPENT	MONEY RECEIVED	BALANCE

NOTES: _____
_____
_____
_____

STARTING BALANCE: _____

DATE	DESCRIPTION	MONEY SPENT	MONEY RECEIVED	BALANCE

NOTES: _____

_____

_____

_____

STARTING BALANCE:

DATE	DESCRIPTION	MONEY SPENT	MONEY RECEIVED	BALANCE

NOTES: _____

_____

_____

_____

STARTING BALANCE:

DATE	DESCRIPTION	MONEY SPENT	MONEY RECEIVED	BALANCE

NOTES: _____

_____

_____

_____

STARTING BALANCE:

DATE	DESCRIPTION	MONEY SPENT	MONEY RECEIVED	BALANCE

NOTES: _____

_____

_____

_____

STARTING BALANCE:

DATE	DESCRIPTION	MONEY SPENT	MONEY RECEIVED	BALANCE

NOTES: _____

_____

_____

_____

STARTING BALANCE:

DATE	DESCRIPTION	MONEY SPENT	MONEY RECEIVED	BALANCE

NOTES: _____

_____

_____

_____

STARTING BALANCE:

DATE	DESCRIPTION	MONEY SPENT	MONEY RECEIVED	BALANCE

NOTES: _____

_____

_____

_____

STARTING BALANCE:

DATE	DESCRIPTION	MONEY SPENT	MONEY RECEIVED	BALANCE

NOTES: _____

_____

_____

_____

STARTING BALANCE:

DATE	DESCRIPTION	MONEY SPENT	MONEY RECEIVED	BALANCE

NOTES: _____

_____

_____

_____

STARTING BALANCE:

DATE	DESCRIPTION	MONEY SPENT	MONEY RECEIVED	BALANCE

NOTES: _____

_____

_____

_____

STARTING BALANCE:

DATE	DESCRIPTION	MONEY SPENT	MONEY RECEIVED	BALANCE

NOTES:_____

_____

_____

_____

STARTING BALANCE:

DATE	DESCRIPTION	MONEY SPENT	MONEY RECEIVED	BALANCE

NOTES: _____

_____

_____

_____

STARTING BALANCE:

DATE	DESCRIPTION	MONEY SPENT	MONEY RECEIVED	BALANCE

NOTES: _____

_____

_____

_____

STARTING BALANCE:

DATE	DESCRIPTION	MONEY SPENT	MONEY RECEIVED	BALANCE

NOTES: _____

_____

_____

_____

STARTING BALANCE:

DATE	DESCRIPTION	MONEY SPENT	MONEY RECEIVED	BALANCE

NOTES: _____

_____

_____

_____

STARTING BALANCE:

DATE	DESCRIPTION	MONEY SPENT	MONEY RECEIVED	BALANCE

NOTES: _____

_____

_____

_____

STARTING BALANCE:

DATE	DESCRIPTION	MONEY SPENT	MONEY RECEIVED	BALANCE

NOTES: _____

_____

_____

_____

STARTING BALANCE:

DATE	DESCRIPTION	MONEY SPENT	MONEY RECEIVED	BALANCE

NOTES: _____

_____

_____

_____

STARTING BALANCE:

DATE	DESCRIPTION	MONEY SPENT	MONEY RECEIVED	BALANCE

NOTES:_____

_____

_____

_____

STARTING BALANCE:

DATE	DESCRIPTION	MONEY SPENT	MONEY RECEIVED	BALANCE

NOTES: _____

_____

_____

_____

STARTING BALANCE: _____

DATE	DESCRIPTION	MONEY SPENT	MONEY RECEIVED	BALANCE

NOTES: _____

_____

_____

_____

STARTING BALANCE:

DATE	DESCRIPTION	MONEY SPENT	MONEY RECEIVED	BALANCE

NOTES: _____

_____

_____

_____

STARTING BALANCE:

DATE	DESCRIPTION	MONEY SPENT	MONEY RECEIVED	BALANCE

NOTES: _____

_____

_____

_____

STARTING BALANCE:

DATE	DESCRIPTION	MONEY SPENT	MONEY RECEIVED	BALANCE

NOTES: _____

_____

_____

_____

STARTING BALANCE:

DATE	DESCRIPTION	MONEY SPENT	MONEY RECEIVED	BALANCE

NOTES: _____

_____

_____

_____

STARTING BALANCE:

DATE	DESCRIPTION	MONEY SPENT	MONEY RECEIVED	BALANCE

NOTES: _____

_____

_____

_____

STARTING BALANCE:

DATE	DESCRIPTION	MONEY SPENT	MONEY RECEIVED	BALANCE

NOTES: _____

_____

_____

_____

STARTING BALANCE:

DATE	DESCRIPTION	MONEY SPENT	MONEY RECEIVED	BALANCE

NOTES: _____

_____

_____

_____

STARTING BALANCE:

DATE	DESCRIPTION	MONEY SPENT	MONEY RECEIVED	BALANCE

NOTES: _____
_____
_____
_____

STARTING BALANCE:

DATE	DESCRIPTION	MONEY SPENT	MONEY RECEIVED	BALANCE

NOTES: _____

_____

_____

_____

STARTING BALANCE:

DATE	DESCRIPTION	MONEY SPENT	MONEY RECEIVED	BALANCE

NOTES: _____
_____
_____
_____

STARTING BALANCE:

DATE	DESCRIPTION	MONEY SPENT	MONEY RECEIVED	BALANCE

NOTES: _____

_____

_____

_____

STARTING BALANCE:

DATE	DESCRIPTION	MONEY SPENT	MONEY RECEIVED	BALANCE

NOTES: _____

_____

_____

_____

STARTING BALANCE:

DATE	DESCRIPTION	MONEY SPENT	MONEY RECEIVED	BALANCE

NOTES: _____

_____

_____

_____

STARTING BALANCE:

DATE	DESCRIPTION	MONEY SPENT	MONEY RECEIVED	BALANCE

NOTES: _____

_____

_____

_____

STARTING BALANCE:

DATE	DESCRIPTION	MONEY SPENT	MONEY RECEIVED	BALANCE

NOTES: _____
_____
_____
_____

STARTING BALANCE:

DATE	DESCRIPTION	MONEY SPENT	MONEY RECEIVED	BALANCE

NOTES: _____

_____

_____

_____

STARTING BALANCE:

DATE	DESCRIPTION	MONEY SPENT	MONEY RECEIVED	BALANCE

NOTES: _____

_____

_____

_____

STARTING BALANCE:

DATE	DESCRIPTION	MONEY SPENT	MONEY RECEIVED	BALANCE

NOTES: _____

_____

_____

_____

STARTING BALANCE:

DATE	DESCRIPTION	MONEY SPENT	MONEY RECEIVED	BALANCE

NOTES: _____

_____

_____

_____

STARTING BALANCE:

DATE	DESCRIPTION	MONEY SPENT	MONEY RECEIVED	BALANCE

NOTES: _____
_____
_____
_____

STARTING BALANCE:

DATE	DESCRIPTION	MONEY SPENT	MONEY RECEIVED	BALANCE

NOTES: _____

_____

_____

_____

STARTING BALANCE:

DATE	DESCRIPTION	MONEY SPENT	MONEY RECEIVED	BALANCE

NOTES: _____

_____

_____

_____

STARTING BALANCE:

DATE	DESCRIPTION	MONEY SPENT	MONEY RECEIVED	BALANCE

NOTES: _____

_____

_____

_____

STARTING BALANCE:

DATE	DESCRIPTION	MONEY SPENT	MONEY RECEIVED	BALANCE

NOTES: _____

_____

_____

_____

NOTES

NOTES

NOTES

NOTES

NOTES

NOTES

NOTES

NOTES

NOTES

NOTES

Made in the USA
Las Vegas, NV
25 June 2022